Trong's H...

Karen J. Guralnick
Illustrated by Winson Trang

Characters

 Ms. Bowman   Trong

 Mai   Parker

 Phu   Lan

 Mom   Dad

Rigby • Saxon • Steck-Vaughn

www.HarcourtAchieve.com
1.800.531.5015

Ms. Bowman: Please take your notebooks out. For homework, I want each of you to write about your hero.

 Mai: What is a hero?

 Ms. Bowman: A hero is someone who you think does great things.

Trong: Is a hero someone famous?

Ms. Bowman: Sometimes a hero is a famous person.

Trong: Who are you going to write about, Parker?

Parker: I don't know yet.

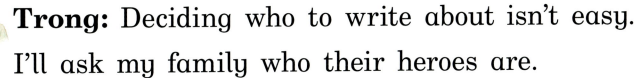 **Trong:** Deciding who to write about isn't easy. I'll ask my family who their heroes are.

Dad: Trong, do you have any homework?

Trong: Yes, my homework is to write about my hero.

Trong: Phu, who is your hero?

Phu: My hero is Samuel Bravo. I think he is the best baseball player in the world.

Trong: Lan, who is your hero?

 Lan: I like Claire Pierre, and all my friends like her, too. She always runs onto the stage, singing her best.

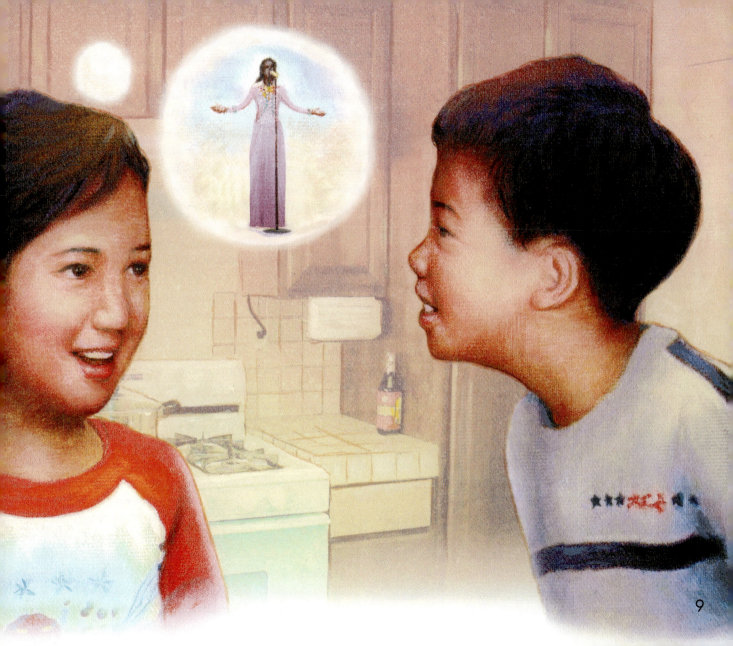

Trong: Who is your hero, Dad?

 Dad: Kai Pham is my hero.

 Trong: Who is Kai Pham?

 Dad: He is a great actor from Vietnam.

11

Mom: My hero isn't a famous person.

Trong: Who is your hero, Mom?

Mom: My hero is Mrs. Yoder. She is a wonderful neighbor who always helps people.

Trong: Maybe my hero doesn't have to be a famous person, either. My hero can be someone I know!

Dad: Do you know who you will write about, Trong?

Trong: Yes, now I know who my hero is.

Ms. Bowman: Trong, who is *your* hero?

Trong: My hero is my mom.

Trong: My mom came to the United States, and she didn't speak English. Now her job is teaching English to Vietnamese students.

 Ms. Bowman: Wow, Trong, your mom *is* a hero!